Career As An Actor

What They Do, How to Become One, and What the Future Holds!

Brian Rogers

KidLit-O Books

www.kidlito.com

Table of Contents

About KidCaps

KidLit-O is an imprint of BookCaps™ that is just for kids! Each month BookCaps will be releasing several books in this exciting imprint. Visit are website or like us on Facebook to see more!

Actress Jenna Fischer signs autographs for her fans[1]

1 http://www.adelaidenow.com.au/ipad/office-life-goes-on-for-jenna-fischer/story-fn6ci13q-1226064705446

Introduction

Jenna Fischer looked at the line of people that stretched before her. Their faces were full of smiles, and the bright flashes from all the cameras was slightly disorienting. As she began to walk down the red carpet towards the theater, people waiting on the sides stuck out their hands for her to shake, tried to take pictures with her, and held out photos and scraps of paper for her to sign. Jenna smiled, put her arms around the people she took pictures with, signed photos of her own face, and tried to say something nice to each person that she met. Before long, Jenna felt her manager pulling her along, reminding her that she was already late to get her seat inside the theater. With a final wave and a blown kiss to her fans, Jenna turned away from the screaming crowd and entered into the large theater where the awards presentation was about to take place.

As she walked into the hushed theater, which seemed like a thousand miles away from the madness outside, Jenna reflected back on the 12 years that had passed since she had moved to Los Angeles from St. Louis, Missouri. When she had first arrived in the big city, she had known that things would be tough economically. She had thought that maybe even a whole year would go by before she got her first paying job as an actress and that, in the meantime she would probably have live a simple life and work nights as a waitress or something. However, it wasn't long before many months had passed, and still no significant acting roles had come her way. She even had to share an apartment with a friend from college just to save some money, and they had to hang an old sheet over the window because curtains were too expensive.

In the meantime, Jenna had tried to stay busy. She acted in local plays and even got to meet a playwright once. But the playwright, instead of encouraging Jenna to pursue her dream of acting, told her: "You aren't a real actress…You aren't going to make it in this town. You should just go home."[2] Can you imagine how those words made her feel?

But Jenna didn't give up. Although three more years would pass before she got her first speaking role on a TV show, Jenna kept going to auditions, acting in community theatre, and trying to improve her acting skills. But in 2005, her seventh year after having moved to LA, Jenna finally got the opportunity of a lifetime-playing a main character on a new NBC sitcom named "The Office". How did she get the part? Even though she didn't get many parts during all those years of showing up to auditions, Jenna did earn the respect of one of the people in

[2] Quotation source: http://tinyurl.com/6m3sgs9

charge of choosing which actors would work in certain shows. So when this new opportunity came along, Jenna was actually invited to go and audition for a role in "The Office". After her audition, everybody loved her, and she soon became an international star.

Jenna had worked tremendously hard to get to where she was. Sometimes it was still hard for her to believe that other people knew her name and that anyone wanted her autograph. But even if it seemed like all of her dreams had already come true, Jenna knew that she would never stop working. At the end of the day, she loved her job. She loved being an actress.

Would you like to have a life like Jenna Fischer's? Would you like to act in films and on television, playing different characters and telling those characters' captivating stories to the world? If so, then maybe the career of a professional actor is for you. Actors are special because they entertain us and can make us think about how we are living our lives. Actors can show us what life was like a thousand years ago or how it may be in the future, and they and can help us to forget about our own problems for an hour or two.

Today, there are all kinds of actors, and there are lots of opportunities for anyone who is willing to dedicate the time and effort necessary towards telling a story well. In this handbook, which is divided into seven sections, we will have a realistic look at what being an actor is all about. We will talk about both the good and the bad in order to help you decide if this is the career that you want to pursue.

In the first section of this handbook, we will talk about what an actor does and how many different kinds of actors are out there. We will also see how much money an actor can expect to make, from their first role all the way until they hit the big time.

The second section will show us some of the intense training that actors must receive before they can get their first paying job. While each individual actor goes down a unique path, most professional actors go through the same basic steps in order to learn and master the craft of acting. And like any new skill, you will see that becoming a talented actor requires dedication and lots of hard work.

Then the third section will answer the question: "Is being an actor an easy job?" Well, as you can probably imagine, the answer you get will depend a lot on who you ask. If you were to ask a brain surgeon or a construction worker what they thought of actors, they may think that being an actor is the easiest thing in the world to do. But as we will see, actors have some unique challenges to meet as part of their job, and not just anyone can do what an actor does.

The fourth section will walk us through the average day in the life of an actor as they prepare for and put on a show. We will look at three different types of actors and see how each one spends their day. We will also learn that, no matter what kind of actor a person chooses to be, there is one golden rule that they can never ignore.

The fifth section will tell us what the hardest part of being an actor is. While being an actor is certainly not an easy job, there are three conditions that come with this career that scare away many people from it. What are these three conditions and how have successful actors learned to deal with them? We will find out.

Then the sixth section will show us what the future of acting holds. In ten years or so, maybe around the time that you may decide to become an actor, what kind of jobs may be available and what will the career of acting be like? We will listen to two professionals in the film industry explain what big changes they think we may see in the near future and how these changes will affect actors.

Finally, the seventh section will talk about what you can do right now in order to get ready to be an actor. While you won't qualify for many auditions while you are still a kid, there are several things that you can do right now to develop certain skills and qualities that every successful actor needs. The sooner that you can learn to put into practice the suggestions in this section, the quicker you will qualify to be an actor, whether on the stage or the screen.

Actors can make us forget about our problems, and they entertain us and make us love them-even though we may never meet them face to face. Are you ready to learn more about this career and the fascinating people who do it? Then let's get started with the first section.

Chapter 1: What Is An Actor?

Thespis, a famous actor from about 2,600 years ago[3]

---

3 http://www.rome101.com/Topics/Herculaneum/Papyri/pages/051111_0954WS.htm

Quick, what's your favorite movie? Is it a cartoon from Disney, a scary movie, or maybe even a sports comedy? What is your favorite scene in that movie? What did the actor/actress do in that scene that impressed you so much?

For a very long time, actors have been entertaining audiences and making them feel certain emotions. The career of acting itself has a very long and interesting history. While people have always liked to tell each other stories and to make each other laugh, at one point people in ancient Greece (and later Rome) decided to build special theaters where anyone could go and watch a show. Most early shows were groups of people (called a "chorus") saying lines together and simply telling a story. But the man in the picture at the beginning of this section, named Thespis, is said to be the first person to have individual actors say lines as the character would say them instead of simply saying words as part of a whole chorus. He was also the first to use masks so that the audience could tell the different characters apart one from the other. The plays of Thespis became so famous that he began to travel from one place to another, carrying masks and costumes on a little wagon.

Since then, on stages in large theaters and on TV and film, actors have used masks, makeup, wigs, and costumes to become totally different people. They often talk, walk, and move differently as part of the role, and a good actor soon makes the audience forget that they are watching a show and makes them start focusing on the story.

A good actor is in the most basic sense, a storyteller. However, instead of simply *telling* us a story, actors *show* us how the story happened. They put themselves into the middle of the story and become one of the characters. And whether an actor is telling us about something that really happened or they are making up a new story, they try to show us the emotions, thoughts, and actions of each character.

Today, actors can be found in one of the three “mediums” (places where shows are seen) that we mentioned earlier: on TV, in the movies, or on the stage. While each medium requires different skills and abilities, it is not rare to see an actor move from one medium to another, slightly changing the way they act for each new role. But even within the three mediums, there are different ways to act.

Most of the time, when people think of actors, they think of the person called the “leading man” or the “leading lady”. For example, in the movie *Titanic*, those would be the characters played by Leonardo DiCaprio and Kate Winslet. In the movie *Twilight*, those would be the character played by Robert Pattinson and Kristen Stewart. But actors can be found in many different areas.

For example, there are actors who play the best friend, the father, the mother, the boss, the coworker, and the mailman delivering letters to the leading man or lady. There are also actors called “stuntmen” who jump off of buildings, drive cars around city streets at high speeds and fight with the main character in dark alleys. There are even actors who don’t say anything at all, but who walk around in the background of the scenes of a film or play to make the setting look more natural.

All of these different actors have learned the skills to do their jobs. But how much money do they earn? Well, actors who work in the background of movies and TV shows are called “extras” or “background actors” and they make around $50 to $100 for an 8 hour day of work, and maybe a little more if they have to work overtime. While they may not get a lot of time on screen, extras do get to hang out on the set or stage, meet celebrities, and learn about the entertainment industry from the inside.

As a background actor develops their abilities, they may get special roles where they can speak a few lines of dialogue or interact directly with the main actors. Even in a minor role, an actor with a few lines can expect to make $500 or more per day. If they become a regular on a television show, then a professional negotiator (called an "agent") will represent the actor and work out some form of regular payment-which may be as much as $10,000 per episode!

If an actor has shown a large amount of talent in different areas and it is clear that the world loves them, then production studios will be willing to pay a lot more money to have that actor be a part of their production because they know that more viewers will pay to see the show, whether it is on stage, TV, or on the big screen. The more popular the actor and the production are, the more money that the actor can expect to receive. For example, a terrific character actor on the stage in a Broadway show can expect to earn about $3,000 per week while a leading role can get them $10,000 or more per week. Of course, as we will see later, stage actors and film actors earn every cent of the money they get by putting in long days filled with sweat and hard work.

Leading men and ladies in film and TV have some of the most impressive salaries because the entire world is willing to pay to see them act. A recent TV hit in the United States called "The Big Bang Theory" saw the three main actors (Jim Parsons, Johnny Galecki, and Kaley Cuoco)earning $350,000 per episode for the seventh season of their show. Because each season has 24 episodes, it means that these actors can expect to make $8.4 million for *one year* of work.

In big-budget movies, leading men and ladies can also expect to make lots of money. For example, Johnny Depp earned $35 million for his role of Captain Jack Sparrow in *Pirates of the Caribbean: On Stranger Tides*, while Will Smith made $20 million for his role as Agent J in *Men in Black 3*. After making one blockbuster after another, it's no wonder that some actors eventually make enough money to build large homes and even to buy their own private island!

Actors have learned to successfully market themselves to casting directors when auditioning for new parts. For every audition, they have to make it clear that they are a serious person who can be relied upon to get the job done. And even if they don't get a particular role, like Jenna Fischer they can earn a strong reputation that might get them an even better role in the future.

Chapter 2: What Is the Training Like to Become An Actor?

Students learning how to act[4]

Every job requires some kind of training. Doctors and lawyers have to spend many years at their local university learning about the human body or the law where they live. Even waiters and

[4] Image source: http://m0delingagency.wordpress.com/page/2/

French fry cooks need to learn the basics of how to get their jobs done. Being an actor is no different, although there are some very specific things that every actor needs to learn.

If you are interested in becoming an actor, or at least wondering if it might be a good option for you to think about, then you would probably like to know what kind of training you should plan for. Being an actor involves three main kinds of training: FORMAL, INFORMAL, and ON THE JOB training. Let's look at each of these three categories to see what actors learn and how they learn it.

FORMAL TRAINING: Many hopeful actors start learning about their craft while still in high school by joining the drama club or a film class and acting in plays and short films after school. They learn about different kinds of theater, how to show emotions, the history of acting, and even the basics of wearing makeup and costumes.

But for most professional actors, the real education begins once they go to college.

Many colleges offer some sort of a program to earn a Bachelor of Arts degree in Theater. Like in the picture at the beginning of this section, students are often given a script and then asked to perform a scene from it. They may be asked to show strong emotion, like love, jealousy, anger, or sadness. Then, their professor and fellow students will give them practical suggestions on how they can improve their acting. While it may not be easy for an actor to hear criticism about the way that they act, it is a hugely important part of learning and getting better. Some actors may even choose to attend a special school that just teaches acting, although schools like that can be terribly hard to get into and quite expensive.

INFORMAL TRAINING: Apart from taking acting classes, actors can learn a lot of things on their own. For example, many acting experts recommend that to become a great actor you need to watch other great actors. So no matter what kind of acting they hope to do (stage, TV sitcom, stuntman, big-budget action movie) actors try to watch other successful actors to see what kinds of things they can learn. For example, student actors may focus on the face of an experienced actor as he or she says their lines. Where is the actor looking? Are their eyebrows moving? Students also look at the actor's body language and hand movements. While experienced actors don't make any movement unless it adds to the scene, actors with less experience will often move their hands and arms way too much and end up looking silly.

Acting experts also recommend that actors try to be extremely observant of everyday people as they go about living their lives. So new actors try to watch how their friends and family act when they are happy or worried, or even when they are sad. They notice how their shoulders go up or down, how they clench their jaw, and how they nervously play with their fingers or jewelry. Paying attention to and imitating all of these little details are what make the difference between a terrific actor and a "so-so" actor.

ON THE JOB TRAINING: Finally, actors can learn a lot by getting out there and acting. Just like you can't learn everything about riding a bicycle until you actually jump on one and start pedaling, there are certain things about acting that can't be taught in a book. So many actors, even if they don't have a paid job yet, try to stay busy getting better and better at their craft. They join local community theater groups and work backstage and in small roles without earning a dime. They act in college and independent films, just happy to be doing what they love and not worrying too much about how much money they make while doing it.

For a new actor, though, there are plenty of traps. New actors may be approached by people who claim to be very important in the acting industry but who will actually want to take advantage of the new actor. People like this may tell the new actor lies and promise them lots of money and fame or they may try to get the actor or actress to do some bad things with the promise that it will help the actor to get a decent role in the future. People like that are simply predators who do not really want to help new actors. Instead of giving their time and money to bad guys like that, each new actor should focus on improving their skills and on attending lots of auditions because that is the only sure way to find success.

Chapter 3: Is Being An Actor An Easy Job?

Actors are often seen relaxing on large boats and beautiful beaches[5]

When you see pictures of actors lying in the sun on a private yacht or floating in a large swimming pool behind their mansion, do you imagine that actors' lives are incredibly easy and that they just get to relax and lie around twenty-four hours a day? Well, while not all actors are the same, in

[5] Image source: http://www.therichest.com/world/the-top-10-celebrities-with-the-nicest-yachts/

most cases they have had to work exceptionally hard for every dollar that they have.

While being an actor may at times pay a lot of money (especially in the case of leading men and ladies) the job also has some unique challenges that not everyone can handle. In this section, we will have a look at four very specific challenges that actors have to meet as part of their job. After we have examined them, you will be able to decide for yourself whether or not being an actor is an easy job.

The first challenge has to do with something that every actor must do before they can start working professionally: they must move to a new city. In the case of stage actors, most of them must move to New York City while in the case of film and television actors, most of them must move to Los Angeles. It's not easy for everyone to make such a big move like that. Think about Jenna Fischer, whose story we saw at the beginning of this handbook. When she arrived in Los Angeles, she actually only knew one person: her future roommate. Other than that, she had left her friends and family behind in St. Louis, Missouri, which was about 1,800 miles away. Can you imagine doing something like that?

Moving to a new city can be pretty tough, because you don't know which neighborhoods are safe, where to look for work, which restaurants are good, and so on. But, like Jenna Fischer, with time most actors learn their way around the city and are able to adapt. And although it may take several years before getting their first acting job, they are determined to hang in there and not to give up.

The second challenge faced by actors in their jobs has to do with working unusually long hours. In the case of stage actors, they must perform an average of five or six plays per week, and the time in between is filled with rehearsals.

In the case of big-budget films, the actor must put up with a hectic schedule that can last for two or three months. The actors are often required to travel far away from their families while shooting scenes for the film. Because movie studios and directors work with tight deadlines, they only have a certain amount of time to complete all of the filming of a movie or television show. So if there are any problems, then the actors must work late into the night until they have gotten the scenes just right.

For television shows, the actor's schedule never quite slows down. Except for a month or two during the summer, most actors have to keep up the busy schedule of working around the clock in order to get the show ready on time and to perform it for the audience. Their days are filled with rehearsing new scenes, training with new cast members, trying on costumes, standing in the right areas for the lighting crew to make adjustments, and finally putting on the show.

A third unique challenge for actors is learning to dedicate themselves wholly to their roles. Sometimes, they must show the emotions of the character, and be ready to scream, yell, or even cry as part of the story. Can you imagine focusing so much on what the character is feeling that you start to feel the same things?

Other actors must change the way that their body looks for a certain role. For example, Tom Hanks had to lose about 50 pounds for his role of a man trapped on a deserted island in *Castaway*. Can you imagine doing something like that? Christian Bale, meanwhile, lost 62 pounds for his role of a disturbed man in *The Machinist*. For several months before shooting the film, he only ate an apple or a can of tune per day along with some coffee. His self-control helped him to lose all that weight. But then, for his next film, *Batman Begins*, he gained back all of the weight he has lost (plus an additional 40 pounds) to look like a big and strong hero. Do you think that you could be so disciplined and change your body to look like each new character that you play?

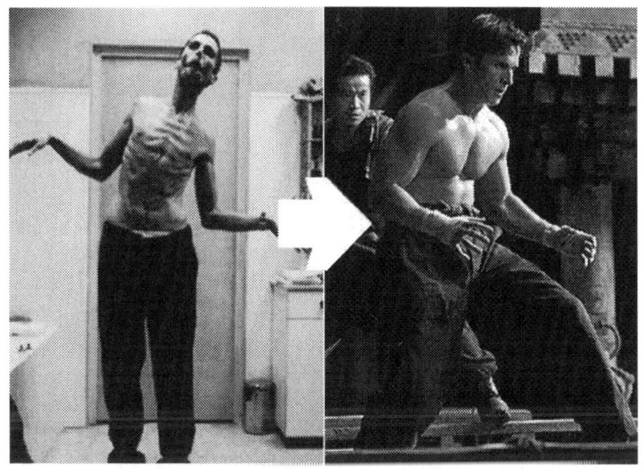

Christian Bale dedicates himself to the roles that he plays[6]

Do you think that just anyone has that type of willpower and the ability to stay so focused on something? In order to lose so much weight,

[6] Image source: http://www.thisis50.com/profiles/blogs/weight-loss-stories-of-actors

both Tom Hanks and Christian Bale had to control their diets for several months. Do you think that you could put forth so much effort to really *become* the character that you are trying to portray?

Finally, many actors have to deal with something which is called "typecasting". Have you ever heard that word before? "Typecasting" is where an actor only gets invited to audition for certain types of characters. For example, an older man might only get roles where he has to be the grandfather to the leading man. An actor with a funny voice might only get roles as the villain (the bad guy) in a film or play. Why can typecasting be frustrating for some actors?

Most actors choose their career because they want to be storytellers. In school, they loved the fact that each new role challenged them and asked them to do something different. But if they are ever typecast, then some actors may feel bored and feel that directors won't take them seriously and doubt that the actor has the ability to act in any other type of role. Some actors even get mightily upset if they are asked to play the same role over and over.

But some other actors decide not to fight being typecast and are happy to just keep doing what they love. They make it their goal to give better and better performances each time, even if the characters are similar.

These four challenges are unique to the world of acting, but many actors have been able to overcome them and to keep working as entertainers for many years.

Chapter 4: What Is the Average Day Like For An Actor?

While no two acting jobs are exactly alike, there are some similarities that most actors experience. Let's have a look at three different kinds of actors and see what a day in their life is like.

A film extra: As we saw earlier, the job of a film extra is to blend into the back of a scene to give it life. An extra is not supposed to distract the attention of the audience away from what the main actors are doing or saying. While waiting for the actual shooting to begin, extras often have to wait for several hours.

The day of a film extra normally begins with them driving to the location of shooting. Once there, they will check in with a key person and then go to the wardrobe and makeup areas to see if there are any special needs for the scene. For example, if the movie is supposed to be set in the Old West, then the extras can't walk around wearing sneakers and talking on their smartphones. Once they have their clothes and makeup prepared, the extras go to a waiting area and kind of just hang out until the director is ready for them.

Once the time comes, the extras will go to their positions and wait for the director to yell "Action!" Then, they will carry out a certain action while the main characters film the scene. They may pretend to wash dishes, drive a car, play with their kids, eat food, walk across the street; practically anything that you can imagine. In some large fight scenes, large numbers of extras must pretend to fight and fall on the ground while the main characters speak their lines and act out their parts.

Once the day's scenes are finished being filmed, the extras can go home. In between takes, extras can grab some of the food that has been set out for them, and they may even have a chance to speak with some of the other workers on the set, including cameramen, lighting directors, and principal actors. If there are any problems with the scene, then the background actors may end up spending more than eight hours on the set, which means that they will get paid a little extra for working overtime. Most extras like to bring a book to read or something to do so that they don't get bored while waiting for the shooting to start.

A stage actor: A stage actor usually has to perform the same show five or six times per week. So each evening, Tuesday through Sunday, they know that they will be on stage speaking, singing, and maybe even dancing in front of a crowd of thousands of people. But when they aren't performing, what do stage actors do with their time?

Most stage actors have their mornings to themselves, but they must be at the studio by 10 AM for rehearsals. Even if they have been performing the same play for months, there are always small details to improve upon and change. For example, the first few hours of each rehearsal may focus on singing better as a group, on getting the timing just right for entering and exiting the stage, and on complicated dance routines. After group rehearsals, most of the singers, dancers, and main stars will separate to different areas and focus on their individual roles. Sometimes, actors may need some one-on-one instruction with the choreographer (dance instructor) or a vocal coach to make sure that the final performance is just right.

Then, after a short lunch break, the whole cast will often get together for a complete rehearsal of the play, usually in full costume and with the orchestra playing. A rehearsal like this is called "dress rehearsal", and during it the director will stop the performers from time to time in case they need to make any changes or in case a mistake is made. After a long day of rehearsals, practice, and problem solving, the actors will be ready to put on a great performance that evening. Often, the actors won't go home until 10 or 11 PM, meaning that they have spent almost 12 hours working that day. On some days, the cast may even have to perform two shows!

A leading man or lady in a movie: The leading man or lady in a movie has a very demanding schedule because they are expected to be in almost every scene, which means that they have to spend a lot of time learning their lines and making sure that they "hit their marks" (stand in the right place) for each different scene. For action movies, the main actors and actresses must also spend long hours rehearsing fight scenes, stunts, and running, all without hurting themselves or anyone else. Professional actors can make fighting scenes look so real that the audience may almost forget that they are watching a movie.

After arriving at the shooting location (whether at a movie studio, in Hollywood, or even in another country) the leading man or lady will have to make sure that they are dressed and ready by the time the director wants to begin shooting. For highly complex roles, actors may have to be at the makeup and wardrobe department as early as 4 or 5 AM to get ready for their part.

Actor Michael Clarke Duncan had to spend about three hours each day putting on makeup for his role in the 2001 film *The Planet of the Apes*[7]

Normally by around 8 or 9 in the morning, the actors will be expected to be on site and to have their lines memorized. In case they forget a line or two, they can always start the scene over, but it would be unprofessional to forget a lot of lines and to waste everybody's time. The best actors can often shoot entire scenes without making any mistakes at all.

After they shoot their scenes for the day, most actors will spend their evenings in their trailers, temporary little houses rented for them by the studio. The actors will focus on learning their lines for the next day's scenes, they will speak with the director about any problems in their

---

7 Image source: http://www.dvd.reviewer.co.uk/news/interview.asp?Index=5489

performance, and they will call their families back home to let them know how work is going. Some movies require the actors to spend two months or more away from home, shooting on location. While this can be difficult, the resulting piece of art can be truly authentic and moving, something that could never have been achieved in a studio using unique effects.

No matter what kind of actor a person chooses to be (an extra, a stage actor, or a leading man or lady), there is one golden rule that all of them need to learn: “The Director is God”. What does that mean? Even though actors may have many years of experience and may have a certain idea as to how the scene should be acted or what a certain character should act and sound like, at the end of the day the director is the one who has actually been given the job to bring the story to life. The actors are like brushes that the director uses to paint a beautiful picture. But when an actor or actress refuses to listen to the advice or suggestions of the director, there can be some real problems on the set of the production. In fact, some actors can get such a bad reputation that no other directors will want to work with them again in the future.

The average day in the life of an actor is not as glamorous or easy as some people may think. In order to do a great job, there is lots of preparation, work, sweat, and even tears that the audience never sees. But most actors happily do this extra work because they love improving their craft and love giving the audience a spectacular show each and every time.

Chapter 5: What Is the Hardest Part of Being An Actor?

Actors sometimes feel like they are always in the public eye[8]

As we have seen, actors live exciting lives and, despite the challenges, they honestly love what

[8] Image source: http://gossipextra.com/2011/12/22/gossip-extra-paparazzi-onenews-1239/

they do. But as is the case with any job, there are a few conditions that are more than challenging; they are almost *impossible* for some people to deal with. In this section, we will look at three conditions that are hard for actors to deal with and that have convinced some people that being an actor is just not for them. Then we will see how successful actors deal with these difficult aspects of their lives.

1) **Being rejected at auditions.** Even great actors don't always fit the description of what the director is looking for. Often, when an actor shows up to try out for a part in a film, TV show, or play, there are dozens or even hundreds of other people waiting to try out for the same part. There is so much competition and only one person will be able to get the part. So imagine how it feels when, after having practiced for so long, the casting director looks at you and says: "No thank you. Next."

What happened? While some actors may worry that they did something wrong or messed up their lines, in many cases the director is simply looking for a certain type of person. For example, if you are an African-American man, but the director is looking for a Latino woman, no matter how good you act you probably won't get the part. So most actors have learned to remember that while they may not get some parts because of how they look or who they are there will be other parts where they are exactly what the director is looking for. The key is not to take the rejection personally.

2) Not making any money at first. Did you see how little money actors make when they are first starting out? Film and TV extras might only make one or two hundred dollars a day, and other types of acting work (like Community Theater or student films) may not even have paid roles! Like Jenna Fischer, many actors may spend several years living with just a little bit of money and learning to be happy with less than what others have. How do actors stay motivated and not give up during their first few years in Hollywood or New York City?

The key is for an actor to stay focused on their goal and to keep doing what they love. An actor is a type of artist and is a professional storyteller. They want to be paid for doing what they love. So even during the tough days and during the times that they have to get a second or third job to support themselves while trying to land a big role, actors don't give up easily on their dream. Staying busy acting, even if it's in Community Theater, helps keep many actors happy as they continue to learn more and to do what they love. The less they worry about money, the happier most actors are.

3) Always being in the public eye. When you looked at the picture at the beginning of this section, were you impressed with how many cameras there were? Of course, actors know that on festive occasions, there will be lots of cameras. When they are on set, at an awards show, or at a wedding, actors know that photographers may yell their name and try to get them to look in their direction. But can you imagine being followed by people with cameras everywhere you go? Can you imagine having people yell at you and try to talk to you when you go to the store, to the doctor's office, or out to eat with your friends?

Actors have to get used to having people always following them around and trying to get their attention. Some actors get tired of all the attention and start to yell at and fight with the photographers who follow them. Newspapers sometimes try to guess what is going on in the private lives of famous actors, and sometimes the rumors that are printed can make an actor look bad, even if the actor hasn't done anything wrong.

How do famous actors deal with all of this pressure? Most of them simply learn to stay at home more often and to go to places where no one cares who they are. Some actors may even hire bodyguards to keep photographers away from them and their family, but that doesn't always work. Most famous actors just learn to smile and to wave and try to be nice to everyone that they meet. That way, the actor's reputation isn't affected, and they can just go on with their lives.

These three difficult circumstances have made some people decide that they could never become a professional actor. However, for those who have learned to deal with these challenges, a lifetime of entertainment (and high paychecks) awaits them.

Chapter 6: What Does the Future Hold for the Career of An Actor?

Today, there are lots of jobs for actors in TV, theater, and in the movies. While the competition is high, a lot of the competition actually has to do with the directors looking for a particular type of actor, and not so much with the fact that there are too few jobs. But what will the future be like? In ten years or so, what kind of work will actors be doing and what kinds of shows can audiences expect to see?

Two respected names in the entertainment industry are Steven Spielberg and George Lucas, the men whose ideas and hard work brought us films like *Star* Wars, *Indiana Jones,* and *Jurassic Park*.

Steven Spielberg and George Lucas[9]

In June of 2013, Mr. Spielberg and Mr. Lucas were interviewed about what they thought the future of Hollywood may be. While only time will tell if they are right in what they said, these two men certainly have a lot of experience and some interesting ideas. What do they think will happen?

George Lucas thinks that big budget movies will become less common and that people will have

[9] Image source: http://www.movieweb.com/news/george-lucas-and-steven-spielberg-predict-studios-will-implode-and-vod-is-the-future

to pay more money to see blockbuster films in the theater. He imagines that, in the future, people will pay $75 or more to see a film that will stay in the theaters for months, almost like going to see a Broadway show or a sporting event today. He also imagines that lower-budget films and shows will be made for the internet, and not for television.

Steven Spielberg has a slightly different idea of how things will be. He thinks that movies will become more interactive. He thinks that the movie screen separates the viewer from the world of the film, and he imagines that in the future technology will allow a viewer to feel completely surrounded by what is going on in the film. He hopes that viewers will be able to look up, down, and all around and feel like they are in the middle of the action (kind of like how some plays today send their characters out into the audience to speak and interact with the viewers).

If the guesses of Mr. Spielberg and Mr. Lucas are correct, then what might that mean for actors? Well, it may mean more jobs for actors, but it may also mean lower pay at most of those jobs. As fewer big-budget movies are made, it would probably lead to actors making films and television shows for less money. Most actors would be okay with that because they are focused on the job and not so much on the money that they make. Stage actors won't be too affected by these changes. But what about those actors imagined by Mr. Spielberg, the ones who would create a 360° film? They would have to get used to always being on camera, and not on just doing their scene and then walking away and off the set. It would certainly change things.

As more and more films and TV focus on using the internet, it may become less and less common to go and see films in the theater. Does that worry you? Well, a little over a hundred years ago, the only way to see a show was to go and see the actor perform in person. It was only in the 1920s and after that movie theaters become more common, and that people could go see actors anytime they wanted. In the future, things may go back to being how they used to be with it being harder to see actors on film and easier to see them in person in a stage show.

Change isn't always a bad thing. Although it may take some getting used to, new technology may actually help actors and directors to make audiences a greater part of the story. Can you imagine being in the middle of your favorite movie and not just watching it from your seat?

Chapter 7: How Can You Get Ready Now to Be An Actor?

Kids in high school participating in a school play[10]

While you may have to wait a few more years before you can go to college and study acting, there are quite a few things that you can do right

[10] Image source: http://www.fortbendisdnews.com/go/doc/1934/1368551/

now to develop some of the qualities and skills of a professional actor. Of course, you can always join your high school's drama club and learn how to act that way, but there are other ways to prepare yourself for the career of an actor that you may not have thought of. What are they? Have a look at the following list.

1) Learn the basics. Every professional actor has to learn the basics of acting. They must learn how to become the character that they are playing, how to show emotions and how to use their facial expressions and gestures to make the words stronger and more natural. Actors must also learn to identify what strengths they have and how to be in the right place at the right time so that each scene comes out just the way that the director wants. They must also learn to pronounce their words clearly, often in different accents as each role calls for. Why not record yourself acting and ask others how you can improve?

2) Be observant. Great actors have learned from other prominent actors. So spend some time observing how the most successful actors of the stage and screen tell their stories. Learn how they use pauses in between words, change their tone of voice, and cry when the moment is just right. A subscription to a service like Netflix® can expose you to amazing works of art produced over the years. And don't be afraid to look at older movies to see some of the famous actors of the past, like Humphrey Bogart, Lauren Bacall, and Carey Grant. Also, learn to observe people every day to see how they behave under a wide variety of circumstances and emotions.

3) Read. A big part of being a successful actor involves having a strong imagination. One of the best ways to develop a strong imagination is to read lots of different books by many different authors. Learn to immerse yourself in the lives of the characters and to imagine how they look, what they sound like, and even how they smell! If you can develop a strong imagination, then it will be easier for you to bring a character to life when acting.

4) Keep living your life. Real actors don't just wait around hoping for a big break; they spend time with their friends, get involved in the community and keep themselves in excellent physical and emotional shape. So start now by filling up your heart and mind with friends, experiences, and laughter. These memories and connections will make you a more rounded out actor later on and will give you a richer life now. And don't worry about becoming famous- just enjoy each moment of acting. It will be even better if you can wait until you are an adult to become a professional actor because you will develop life skills that you may not get otherwise.

As you can see, there are lots of things that you can do right now to get ready for the life of an actor. Try to enjoy each of these activities, and even if you don't find success right away, don't worry too much. The goal is to remember that you are living your dream and doing what you love. How many people get to say that every day that they go to work?

Conclusion

Wow! We have learned a lot about the career of an actor. Isn't it amazing to see how much work and preparation goes into pursuing this career? What was your favorite part of this handbook? Was it when we saw how actors have to spend hours preparing for fight scenes or was it when we imagined what the future of acting might be like? Let's review some of the most important points we learned so that we don't forget them.

In the first section, we talked about what an actor does and how many different kinds of actors are out there. We saw how since the very first famous actor, Thespis, actors have tried to entertain audience by telling stories. In fact, actors today are called "Thespians" because they are imitating the work of Thespis. But instead of just using their words, actors use their entire body to become a part of the story they are telling. There are actors who do stunts, comedy, romantic movies, stage shows, and big Hollywood blockbusters. Professional actors may make as little money as a couple of hundred dollars a day or as much as millions of dollars per film.

The second section showed us some of the intense training that actors receive before they can get their first paying job. While each individual actor goes down a unique path, most professional actors have taken the same basic steps in order to learn and master the craft of acting. After studying acting in college, they usually move to a big city and begin to spend most of their time auditioning for different roles. Actors often start out with smaller roles and eventually audition for bigger and bigger roles.

The third section answered the question: “Is being an actor an easy job?” As we saw, actors have some truly unique challenges to meet as part of their job, and not just anyone can successfully meet those challenges. Actors must deal with moving to a new city, working long hours away from their families, and dedicating themselves one hundred percent to each character that they play. Did you see how Tom Hanks and Christian Bale even changed the way that they looked in order to play their roles better? Do you think that you could show that same level of commitment?

The fourth section walked us through the average day in the life of an actor as they put on a show. We had a look look at three different types of actors (a film extra, a stage actor, and a leading man/lady) and saw how each one spends their day. Actors spend a lot of time preparing themselves and rehearsing, and in the case of film extras a lot of time is also spent waiting around for the actual filming to begin. And we also learned that no matter what kind of actor a person chooses to be, there is one golden rule that can never be ignored: "The Director is God". Actors who ignore this rule and argue with the director about their performance will not keep working as actors for long!

The fifth section told us what the hardest part is of being an actor. While being an actor is certainly not an easy job, there are three conditions that come with the job that scare away most people from ever even considering pursuing this career. They involve being rejected during auditions, dealing with the low pay when starting out, and living in the public eye. Successful actors have learned to deal with those problems by focusing on doing what they love and not worrying about what they can't control.

Then the sixth section showed us what the future of acting holds. In ten years or so, maybe around the time that you might decide to become an actor, what kind of jobs may be available and what will the career of acting be like? We saw how Steven Spielberg and George Lucas explained how things may change in the future. Mr. Lucas thinks that the focus will be more on internet programs and that there will be fewer big movies and that they will be more expensive to see. Mr. Spielberg, on the other hand, thinks that movies will soon make the audience feel that they are right in the middle of the action and like they are part of the story. If the predictions of the two men come true, it may mean that actors will end up making less money than they do today.

Finally, the seventh section talked about what you can do right now in order to get ready to be an actor. We saw how practicing the mechanics of acting, being observant, reading, and living your life are all important steps to becoming a well-rounded out person and actor.

There is no doubt: being an actor is a glamorous and exciting job. While not every person has the talent or energy to practice this career, those who choose it are rewarded with high salaries and a life of travel- all while doing what they love. Do you think that you have what it takes to be an actor? Then don't waste any more time. Start practicing now so that when you are older you can jump into the world of Hollywood or Broadway!

Made in the USA
Columbia, SC
10 November 2023

25948417R00039